Eswatini His Heritage

Unveiling Africa's Last Absolute Monarchy

By

Collins Richardson and Abdul-Ghani Karam

Copyright © 2024 by Collins Richardson and Abdul-Ghani Karam. All rights reserved.

Except for brief quotations included in critical reviews and certain other noncommercial uses allowed by copyright law, no part of this publication may be reproduced, distributed, or transmitted in any form or by any means, including photocopying, recording, or other electronic or mechanical methods, without the publisher's prior written permission.

Disclaimer

This book's content is only meant to be used for general informative purposes. The author and publisher do not make any claims or guarantees on the completeness of the material given, despite their best efforts to assure its completeness.

This book is only for informative and educational reasons. It is recommended that readers get guidance from qualified authorities for particular issues or advice on their own health, legal, or financial problems.

Copyright © 2024 by Collins Richardson and Abdul-Ghani Karam

Table of Contents

Table of Contents	3
Introduction	5
Chapter 1	10
Early History of Eswatini	10
Chapter 2	13
The Nation of Swazi	13
Chapter 3	17
Colonial Administration	17
Independent Eswatini	18
Chapter 4	21
Geography of Eswatini	21
Relief and Soils of Eswatini	21
Drainage and Climate	24
Chapter 5	26
Plant and Animal Life	26
Ethnic Groups	27
Settlement Patterns	28
Chapter 6	31
Demographic Patterns	31
Eswatini's Economy	31
Agricultural Practices	32
Chapter 7	34
Industry in Eswatini	34
Trade and Finance	35
Administration in Eswatini	36

Eswatini's Education	38
Health and Welfare	39
Cultural Life	40
Chapter 8	**43**
Heart of Eswatini's Monarchy	43
A Wildlife Haven	43
Protecting Endangered Species	44
A Conservation Pioneer	44
A Landscape of Wonders	45
Chapter 9	**46**
Blend of Nature and Culture	46
Rich biodiversity	47
Riverside safari	47
Celebration of Maidenhood	48
A Renewal Ritual	49
Conclusion	49

Introduction

Eswatini, a landlocked nation in southern Africa, tells a story that weaves together ancient heritage, dramatic landscapes, and a distinct cultural identity. The country's origins date back to prehistoric times and were previously known as Swaziland until 2018, when King Mswati III renamed it. Archaeological finds, such as stone tools and rock art, provide insight into early human activity that dates back over 250,000 years. The San people, known for their craftsmanship, created a legacy of rock murals that are now cultural treasures. The entrance of Bantu-speaking clans over two millennia ago established agricultural methods, iron smelting, and cattle keeping, setting the framework for Eswatini's development.

The Dlamini clan, the Swazi people's forebears, rose to prominence in the 18th century. They began arriving around Delagoa Bay in Mozambique and finally established themselves west of the Lubombo Mountains under the reign of King Ngwane III. By the early nineteenth century, Sobhuza I had unified numerous clans into a cohesive political body, implementing novel techniques such as the Zulu age-grade military system. His successor, Mswati II, increased the kingdom's dominance by conquest and alliances, establishing himself as a formidable leader.

However, in the late nineteenth century, the monarchy was challenged by European powers. The discovery of diamonds and gold in neighboring South Africa sparked increased interest in the region. Boer and British disputes resulted in treaties and accords that steadily weakened Swazi sovereignty. Eswatini fell under British rule in 1903, a period of limited development due to aspirations to integrate it into the South African Union. Despite these restraints, the Swazi people maintained their cultural identity and sovereignty.

Eswatini gained independence in 1968 under King Sobhuza II, who reinstated traditional government while navigating modern administrative structures. His six-decade reign provided relative stability and economic progress. Following his death, King Mswati III took the throne amid calls for democratic reform. Efforts to reform governance resulted in the passage of a new constitution in 2005, which preserved the monarchy's major authority.

The country's topography is as varied as its history. Eswatini's landscapes range from the rugged Highveld in the west to the subtropical Lowveld in the east, with rolling hills, fertile plains, and dramatic escarpments. Major rivers such as the

Komati and Usutu support agriculture and vibrant ecosystems. The climate varies with altitude, with temperate temperatures in the highlands and warm, humid weather in the lowlands.

Eswatini's natural beauty is enhanced by its diverse ecosystem. The Highveld and Lubombo regions have lush woodlands, whereas the Lowveld's savannas are home to a diverse range of wildlife. Conservation efforts have resulted in the establishment of reserves like Hlane Royal National Park and Mkhaya Game Reserve, which safeguard endangered species such as rhinos and elephants. The Mantenga Cultural Village exemplifies traditional Swazi life by combining cultural preservation with ecotourism.

Eswatini's identity is still deeply rooted in cultural traditions. Ceremonies like the Umhlanga, or Reed Dance, and the Incwala, a renewal ceremony, honor unity and the monarchy's position as a unifying force. Traditional music and dance, involving instruments such as the kudu horn and reed flute, add to the excitement of these gatherings. Despite the impact of industrialization, Swazi society maintains a strong connection to its roots.

Eswatini's economy is a combination of traditional practices and modern industry. Subsistence farming, based on crops like maize and sorghum, coexists with commercial agriculture, which focuses on sugarcane and forestry. Mining, which was formerly important, has dwindled, while tourism has become a crucial business. Visitors are drawn to handicrafts, textiles, and cultural festivals, which help to sustain local economies.

Eswatini's governing system combines traditional power with contemporary systems. The Swazi National Council advises the king on customary and constitutional matters. A bicameral legislature has elected lawmakers, but political parties are not allowed. Land ownership is a delicate topic, reconciling communal traditions with modern economic pressures.

Since independence, education and healthcare have grown in popularity, owing to missionary influences. Literacy rates have risen, but obstacles such as HIV/AIDS and insufficient resources remain. The young population, characterized by high birth rates and a strong cultural identity, is both a source of vitality and a need for sustainable development.

Eswatini's story is one of tenacity and celebration of its distinct character. From ancient traditions to modern aspirations, the nation continues to appreciate its legacy while navigating the difficulties of a changing world.

Part 1

History of Eswatini

Chapter 1

Early History of Eswatini

From ancient periods to the present, the history of Eswatini is a study of the noteworthy events and persons in the past. Officially known as the Kingdom of Eswatini (siSwati: Umbuso weSwatini), the nation Eswatini was long known as Swaziland in the colonial period as a protectorate and thereafter as an independent nation; the Anglicized name of an early monarch and nation builder, Mswati II, reigned from 1840 to 1868. In 2018 King Mswati III renamed the nation Eswatini from Swaziland.

Landlocked, Eswatini is bordered by Mozambique and the eastern edge of South Africa. Its greatest dimensions stretch over 110 miles (175km) from north to south and roughly 80 miles (130km) from west to east. Mbabane is the national administrative center.

The Swazi country is a very new political entity; most clan fusion occurred under Dlamini military control about around the middle of the 19th century. But the history of human habitation in what is now Eswatini goes back deep into prehistory. Found on old river terraces, the first stone tools date back more than 250,000 years; subsequent stone tools are linked with evidence of Homo sapiens from maybe as long ago as 100,000 years.

On top of the Ngwenya mountain, people were quarrying red and black hematite ore for cosmetic uses about 42,000 years ago (where in 1964 a large opencut mining operation was established to take advantage of the abundant ore supply). Among the first mining and trade operations in the world, mining persisted for many thousands of years after then. About 20,000 years later, the archeological record shows that the San hunter-gatherers—who produced the unique rock murals scattered across the western portion of the nation—were in residence.

Groups of Bantu-speaking people (Nguni, Sotho, and Tswana) migrated southward over the Limpopo River around 2,000 years ago. Their classification as Early Iron Age people stems from their agricultural activities, animal keeping (sheep and goats), usage of pottery, and smelting of iron. Later on, cows were brought in.

These people are known from Ngwenya, where iron ore mining dates back around 400 CE. These Nguni and Sotho clan forefathers, who the Swazi came across in the late 18th and early 19th centuries, settled more beautiful parts of Eswatini during the next generations.

Part of this southerly migration, the Dlamini clan's forefathers arrived in the Delagoa Bay region of Mozambique some substantial time before the Portuguese arrived in the early 16th century. Until the mid-18th century, the Dlamini ancestors lived as members of the Thembe-Tonga group of people; then, most likely due to dynastic warfare, they migrated southward over the coastal plain between the mountains and the Indian Ocean—"scourging the Lubombo," as a royal praise song puts it.

They referred to themselves as Emalangeni up to this point, after Langa, an ancient chief. Later they migrated westward over the Lubombo mountain and into the Pongola valley, under their king Ngwane III, when about 1770 they founded the first Swazi nation's (bakaNgwane) nucleus close to what is now Nhlangano.

Chapter 2

The Nation of Swazi

In the history of southeast Africa, this was a stormy time when many big clan groups battled for dominance. Two of them, the Ndwandwe and the Zulu, who lived south of the new Ngwane region, seriously threatened the Dlamini, who aimed to rule the tribes among whom they had established. Still, they had made great progress in integrating some of these clans and building relationships with others to form a new political coalition by the end of the century.

About 1820, under their new king, Sobhuza I, also known as Somhlohlo ("The Wonder"), they migrated northward to create a safer stronghold in central Eswatini, as their new power base was insufficient to stifle hostility from their southern neighbors. Part of this achievement may be ascribed to Sobhuza's adoption of the Zulu age-group system of military organization, which established regiments across clan allegiance and was always well disciplined.

The Dlamini solidified their authority under Sobhuza I and his son Mswati II. By 1860, they had expanded their influence via invasion and assimilation far beyond the borders of modern Eswatini under Mswati II, whose name the country bears and who following generations praised as "their greatest fighting king."

But at the height of their might, a new element had surfaced in the regional geopolitics that over the following forty years would lead Swazi territorial and political authority to progressively shrink. Especially after the discovery in South Africa of diamonds in 1867 and gold in 1871, this was the conflicting pressure from the developing Boer republic of the Transvaal and from the increasing British imperial presence.

The inflow into the nation of European prospectors and concession seekers, which the Swazi were able to manage for a while but which turned into a torrent once the kingdom passed to Mbandzeni in 1875, was the primary destabilizing factor.

By 1890, so many concessions had been issued for so many various purposes—in addition to land and mineral rights—that almost the whole nation was covered two, three, or even four thick in concessions of all types and for varying periods of time. As they subsequently found out, the Swazi had signed away their freedom, even though they insisted that they were all leasehold rights with termination date some future.

Granting a charter of conditional self-government subject to the royal veto, the Swazi attempted in 1888 to control the impact of the European migration. Behind the personal struggle for concessions, however, was the intrigue and rivalry of the two white powers, the Boers and the British. The latter tried to confine the former; the former required a path to the sea. The territory the Swazi lived in stood in front of each of them as something to shape.

A pact between the British government and the South African Republic established a temporary administration in 1890 including officials of the two powers along with a Swazi delegate. The British government signed a new convention in 1893 allowing the South African Republic to negotiate with the Swazi regent and her council for a proclamation allowing the republic to assume powers of jurisdiction, legislation, and administration without including Swaziland, as it was then known, into the republic.

The Swazi declined to sign the proclamation, but another pact signed by the two countries in 1894 essentially gave the conditions unilateral force. Following the South African War of 1899–1902, all the rights and powers of the republic transferred to Great Britain; in June 1903, the governor of the Transvaal was permitted to administer Swaziland

and to legislate by declaration by an order in council under the Foreign Jurisdiction Act. These powers were passed to a high commissioner for Swaziland, Bechuanaland, and Basutoland in 1906.

Chapter 3

Colonial Administration

Swaziland sank into a backwater of the British Empire throughout the colonial years 1906 until the late 1940s. A basic reason was that provision had been made in the South Africa Act of 1909 (which formed the Union of South Africa as a British dominion) for the probable ultimate transfer of Swaziland (and Basutoland and Bechuanaland) to the union. Although this prospect existed, little socioeconomic development occurred and it was hard to differentiate Swaziland from the surrounding rural parts of South Africa (border stations).

Politically, the situation was best summed up in the lowering of the king's title to that of paramount chief and of his duty to that of "native administration." Notwithstanding many demands from South Africa over the years, the imperial authorities refused to transfer Swaziland. Events in South Africa after the 1948 election, which marked the beginning of apartheid, strengthened this resolve.

Britain started addressing social issues in Swaziland also from 1945 forward. Although the big apartheid vision of separate homelands for Africans still included Swaziland, the question of transfer was dead by the mid-1950s.

The economy grew briskly from 1960, but sociopolitical development trailed more slowly. Published in 1963, a constitution allowing restricted self-government was adopted; in 1967, the nation became a protected state under which the kingdom was reinstated. On September 6, 1968, complete independence ensued.

Independent Eswatini

1921 saw King Sobhuza II of Swaziland appointed as the ngwenyama of his country. The monarch loved and kept Swazi customs alive. Five years after independence, the monarch reinstated the conventional form of administration in which all effective authority stays in the royal capital by undoing the constitution drafted by the British.

Operating at the grassroots, a form of local administration often called as the tinkhundla Sobhuza's compromise on modern administration was to keep the cabinet structure with a prime minister and other ministers, but the monarch chooses all of them. Under his strict but

18

compassionate leadership, Swaziland had an amazing degree of political stability and economic growth. Emphasizing health, education—which had been overlooked in colonial times—and other human resource advances,

Following the death of King Sobhuza on August 21, 1982, the royal family engaged in a power struggle that was not finally settled until 1986, when the teenage heir, Prince Makhosetive, was appointed King Mswati III. His rule, marked as autocratic and rife with corruption and excess, was beset with demands for democratic reform. Strikes and demonstrations in the 1990s and 2000s aimed at opposing the sluggish advancement toward democratic transformation.

Mswati set up a commission to write a new constitution in 2001 in order to satisfy his many detractors. Published for public review in May 2003, it was attacked for deviating from democratic reform as it forbade opposition political parties and allowed the monarch to keep total controlling authority. Effective in 2006, Mswati signed a revised version in 2005 that neither recognized the existence of political parties nor prohibited ones.

Part 2

Understanding the Land and the People

Chapter 4

Geography of Eswatini

Landlocked on the eastern edge of South Africa, Eswatini is a nation that borders Mozambique. At its greatest proportions, it stretches over 110 miles (175km) from north to south and roughly 80 miles (130km) from west to east.

Originally a protectorate and subsequently an independent nation, Eswatini was long known as Swaziland during the colonial period. Mswati II, an early monarch and country builder with Anglicized name, reigned from 1840 to 1868. Mbabane, the former British colonial government capital, is the administrative center of the nation.

Some 11 kilometers from Mbabane, King Mswati III and his mother live at Phondvo near Lobamba, where the houses of parliament and other national institutions are located. The monarch said in April 2018 that the country's official name would be Kingdom of Eswatini instead of Kingdom of Swaziland.

Relief and Soils of Eswatini

For a tiny nation, a lengthy and convoluted geologic history has produced a terrain with an astonishing range of relief, temperature, and soils. Four clearly defined physiographic areas stretch longitudinally from north to south in fairly parallel strips. From west to east they are the Lowveld, the Middleveld, the Highveld, and the Lubombo (Lebombo) escarpment. Geologically, the youngest formations lie east; the oldest are found in the west.

Covering almost thirty percent of the nation, the complex of granites and more ancient metamorphosed quartzites, sandstones, and volcanics known as the Highveld has been worn into a harsh mountain terrain. The peak massifs of Bulembu (6,108 feet [1,862]) and Ngwenya (5,997 feet [1,828]) in the far west mark the highest points; the average height is between 3,500 and 4,500 feet (1,101 and 1,400 meters). Last to be colonized in the nation, the Highveld was known to the Swazi as Inkangala—a chilly, treeless area. On the softer slopes and in river valleys, its more deeply weathered red to yellow acid soils have emerged.

Comprising around one-fourth of the nation, the Middleveld averages 2,000 to 2,500 feet (610 to 760 meters). There are large, well-watered lowlands and undulating uplands here. It is mostly underlain by ancient granites and gneisses (metamorphosed granites), with dolerites and quartzites, which have weathered deeply to form friable red and clay loams mixed with shallower profiles of sands and sandy loams. To the Swazi, it is the heartland of their country and known as Live ("The Country") or Inkabave ("The Navel).

Covering over 40 percent of the nation, the Lowveld, often known as Bushveld, is a mainly undulating lowland with isolated knolls and hills rising sharply above the 500 to 1,000 foot average.

Generally speaking, the soils reflect the change from the acidic granites and sandstones of the western Lowveld to the more basic basalts and dolerites of the eastern part—i.e., from sandy loams in the west to red and black clays in the east, latter of which are some of the most naturally fertile soils in the nation. The Swazi people refer to this area, Lihlanze, as a warm location with trees—in its natural condition, the usual African savanna.

Comprising a small 600 square mile strip, the Lubombo escarpment and plateau comprise around 5 percent of the nation. Rising suddenly from the Lowveld to an average height of 2,000 feet, it has higher northern peaks (Siteki and Mananga) around 2,500 feet.

The gorges of three of the major rivers running across the nation from west to east—the Umbuluzi, the Usutu, and the Ingwavuma—deeply split it.

Depending on the nature of the volcanic lavas that build the bedrock, the plateau soils vary greatly from shallow sands to deeper loams. The Swazi have no particular name for this region of their nation.

Drainage and Climate

Among southern African nations, Eswatini has among the finest water supplies. With their headwaters in South Africa, major perennial rivers pass across the nation toward the Indian Ocean. They comprise the Lomati, the Komati, the Umbuluzi, and the Usutu. Comprising three major tributaries—the Usushwana, the Ngwempisi, and the Mkhondvo—the Usutu has the greatest watershed in the nation. Rising in western Eswatini and also cutting across the Lubombo, the Ingwavuma rises in the south.

Though mostly subtropical, the country's location on the eastern coast of southern Africa greatly affects the climate because it exposes it to wet marine tropical air flowing off the Indian Ocean for much of the year. Stronger continental winds force marine airflow to stop in winter, which results in high degree of climate variability. The reduction in height of almost 4,000 feet over a space of roughly

50 miles causes the climate to be likewise prone to severe temperature and precipitation gradients from west to east.

On the Highveld, average maximum and lowest monthly temperatures are 72 °F (22 °C) and 52 °F (11 °C); on the Lowveld, they are 84 °F (29 °C) and 59 °F (15 °C). The Middleveld falls on a middle ground among these gradations.

Eswatini is in the subcontinent's summer rainfall zone, where over eighty percent of the precipitation occurs between October and March, mostly in the form of frontal showers and thunderstorms. In the Highveld, average annual rainfall is around 55 inches (1,400 mm; in the Middleveld, 34 inches; in the Lowveld, roughly 22 inches; in Lubombo, 35 inches.

Still, yearly totals vary greatly and numbers have swung drastically from year to year. Within the Middleveld, where most people reside, the average has ranged from a high of 63 inches to a low of 13 inches during a few years. These dramatic variations seem to correspond with wetter and drier than normal quasi-cyclic swings of 8 to 11 years, seen in the rainfall data.

Chapter 5

Plant and Animal Life

The natural vegetation is woodland, primarily limited to the Highveld and the windward slopes of the Lubombo escarpment; savanna and grassland. Variations in vegetation are produced by elements like soil composition and moisture.

From sweet to sour depending on their palatability when mature, there are wet and dry woods, different densities of savanna, and diverse grassland kinds. With ferns and flowering plants alone accounting for more than 2,600 species, overall the flora is abundant. Some species located only in or near Eswatini and have a quite restricted distribution.

Habitat destruction brought on by the human population has seriously depleted the natural fauna in recent years; representative species including antelope (impala, reedbuck, duiker, waterbuck, wildebeest, and kudu) hippopotamus, rhinoceros, elephant, giraffe, and zebra are found mostly in protected reserves. Smaller animals include the baboon, monkey, jackal, and mongoose may still be found, however, and numerous kinds of snakes are also common.

Lowveld rivers also include somewhat many crocodiles. Every ecosystem has a great abundance of birdlife, which consists of resident and migratory (breeding and nonbreeding) groups. From further away (from northern Europe and eastern Asia in the case of storks, swallows, and hawks), the migratory hail central and North Africa. Among the most often occurring birds are Barbets, weavers, several hornbills, the lilac-breasted roller, and the purple-crested loerie.

Ethnic Groups

There are around seventy clans together in the Swazi country. Under the biggest clan, the Dlamini, their leaders follow the customary hierarchy under the ngwenyama and ndlovukazi. Many of the clans of Nguni ancestry that arrived in the nation with the Dlamini in the early 19th century were Sotho-originating, and the merger brought together clans already residing in the now Eswatini.

Recognounced both constitutionally and legally, an uncodified Swazi Law and Custom controls traditional government and culture. Though it shares official status with English, which is in reality used primarily for formal written communication, the language is siSwati, which is like Zulu.

More over four-fifths of the population are Swazis; the rest are immigrants from Mozambique, South Africa, and elsewhere. Among them are several thousand Asians and Europeans and their families working in business.

Settlement Patterns

Mostly in the rural regions, the majority of Swazis are members of Christian churches, both Roman Catholic and Protestant, whose missions were responsible before independence for most of the schooling and medical treatments. Many of their followers, however, also hold the conventional ideas and customs of the rest of the community.

The Swazi people lived in family homesteads scattered throughout the countryside historically. The homesteads of kings and leaders were the only bigger settlements. The introduction of the rural Swazi to the money economy changed this trend in the late 19th century.

Under British colonial control from 1903, nucleated settlements developed at significant administrative and trading hubs; but, the process of urbanization hastened only after World War II, when the development of major agricultural, mining, and industrial operations attracted job seekers and produced sizable company towns including Mhlume, Simunye, Big Bend, and Mhlambanyatsi. The biggest are the commercial and industrial hub of Manzini and Mbabane's administrative center. About one-fifth of the population lives in cities.

The traditional leaders oversee a communal land ownership arrangement for the rural populace. Usually, a homestead consists of the headman's main hut; the huts of his mother, wife (or spouses), and children; the kitchen and storerooms; and the livestock fence front and eastward. Cattle are more than just draft animals and milk producers. They are a stockpile of riches ready for use on social and ceremonial events.

Homestead life follows a rather seasonal rhythm. Women build gardens along the riverbanks when the rains start in spring; later, when the major rains arrive in summer, with men's assistance, they plow or hoe to seed maize and sorghum on bigger fields. All competent women and children leave their homesteads for the fields at this period; the males also participate in weeding and planting. Generally speaking, the summer months are the hungry months—unless remittances from working family members provide otherwise.

Harvest falls from autumn to early winter; by July the last of the sorghum and maize has been dried and hauled in. After that, activity proceeds to the homesteads, where men and women thresh the grain—the finest of which is kept and the rest eaten all at once. Winter offers visiting, hunting, leisure, and entertainment. Population pressure on land, rising drift to the city, lack of men working in the cities, and the use of rented tractors for plowing have somewhat changed this traditional cycle; nonetheless, the overall pattern is still clear.

Both of the historic hubs of Swazi life—the royal villages of the ngwenyama at Ludzidzini and the ndlovukazi at Phondvo—are at the "royal heart" of the nation and not far from the ancient royal capital of Lobamba.

Chapter 6

Demographic Patterns

With approximately one-third between the age of 15 and 29 and more than one-third under the age of 15, Eswatini has a quite youthful population. Women have a greater life expectancy than males; the average for both is around 57 years, much less than the world average.

Although Eswatini's birth and mortality rates are greater than the world average, its population growth rate is somewhat below the global average. The predominance of HIV/AIDS in the adult population helps to explain the shorter life expectancy and population increase rate as well as the higher than normal mortality rate.

Eswatini's Economy

The economy shows a clear dualism in general between small-scale semi-subsistence activities and major intense output. This creates a striking disparity in living conditions and income, which usually goes unnoticed from average per capita figures. Based on the free enterprise or market ideology, national economic policy uses fiscal tools to transfer resources to programs including education, health, and community development. Receipts from the Southern African Customs Union, sales tax, business and personal taxes provide most of government income.

Although the budget is usually in balance, foreign assistance makes a significant contribution to the capital or development budget, therefore acting as a cushion to offset any income shortfall. Still, the parallel economy endures and the official employment sector cannot handle the yearly increase of new workers brought on by the nation's high rate of population increase.

Especially males, many workers are compelled to look for jobs as migrant laborers, especially in South Africa. With a usually divided trade union movement set against a longer-standing employers' association and with the government trying to serve as referee and arbitrator, labour relations in the nation are at an embryonic stage.

Agricultural Practices

Eswatini is engaged in both commercial and subsistence farming mixed together. Among other crops are sorghum (mostly for traditional beer), pumpkins, beans, peas, and various vegetables; maize is the mainstay crop. Though largely poor, more innovative farmers generate on par with the large-scale commercial industry. The number of animals, especially cattle and goats, far exceeds the carrying capacity of the nation and is a main source of vegetation loss and soil erosion because to their traditional usage as a store of wealth.

Growing sugarcane and manufacturing sugar are the two biggest agroindustries. The vast man-made pine and eucalyptus (in the Highveld) man-made woods, which provide lumber to a wood pulp factory and multiple sawmills, have also great economic value. Second biggest export from the nation is unbleached wood pulp, behind sugar.

About six percent of the nation's total territory is covered by wood plantations. Other key crops include rice, tobacco, citrus fruits and cotton (Lowveld), pineapples (Middleveld), and vegetables. Especially in the Lowveld, commercial cattle ranching is very vital and supports dairy plants and meat processing.

Chapter 7

Industry in Eswatini

Since the 1960s, mining has been less important overall, especially with relation to coal and asbestos. Though no mines are presently operational, iron ore, tin, and gold have been sometimes worked in the past. Diamonds have been becoming more and more valuable since 1984; they currently rank second among minerals exported from this country after asbestos.

The core of the industrial sector is the processing of agricultural, forest, and animal goods. Other manufacturers include textiles and apparel, which grew rapidly in the 1980s; drinks, office supplies, furniture, and other light industries.

Particularly from South Africa, tourism has grown to be a key economic industry. Based around the hotel and casino complex in the center Ezulwini valley (approximately seven miles from Mbabane), the sector has smaller complexes at Piggs Peak in the north and Nhlangano in the south. This industry is complemented by a selection of stone and wooden handicrafts and high-quality handcrafted fabrics and tapestries.

Trade and Finance

Comprising Eswatini, Botswana, Lesotho, Namibia, and South Africa, the Southern African Customs Union offers basically for the free flow of products and services within the region. Though it has its own currency, the lilangeni, Eswatini is also a member of the Southern African Monetary Union (with Lesotha and South Africa), which aims to guarantee that currencies are on par and cash flow freely between the members.

Apart from one bank entirely controlled by the government, the commercial banks are divisions of foreign (including South African) institutions. These ties lead most foreign commerce to be with South Africa as part of her regional trading network. While imports include machinery and transportation equipment, fuels and lubricants, and foodstuffs, exports are mostly raw materials or slightly processed goods, largely from the agro-forestry industry.

Good all-weather highways connect the major population hubs to surrounding Mozambique and South Africa. Originally built from the western to the eastern border for the export of iron ore via Maputo in Mozambique, the railway has been expanded to join the South African network both north and south-east of the nation. One international airport serving Eswatini is named after King Mswati III.

Administration in Eswatini

vested in the monarch, executive power is carried out via a double government structure. To assist him in government affairs, the monarch names a cabinet of ministers and a prime minister. Furthermore advising the monarch on all affairs governed by Swazi Law and Custom and in line with Swazi customs and culture is the Swazi National Council. Eswatini's legislative system is bicameral.

There are 65 members of the House of Assembly, ten selected by the monarch and 55 chosen by public ballot. Sometimes the House of Assembly has an extra member if the elected speaker comes from outside that body.

There are thirty senators, ten chosen by the House of Assembly and twenty appointed by the monarch. All people over the age of eighteen combined into 55 constituencies (tinkhundla) make up the general voters. Every tinkhundla chooses one member for the House of Assembly; elections take place at intervals no more than five years. Though numerous are operating in the nation, political parties are outlawed.

Eswatini has a dualistic court system with both conventional and constitutional courts. The constitutional courts consist of an industrial court, the Court of Appeal, the High Court, subordinate or magistrate courts. Traditional Swazi National Courts also exist with two courts of appeal and a higher appeal court. The Swazi National Courts only handle cases wherever all parties engaged are Swazi and the charges fit a limited list of criminal and civil ones. In any instance of dispute between the two systems, they must yield to the constitutional courts.

Local governance is carried out regionally. Appointed by the monarch, an administrator oversees each of the four provinces (Hhohho, Lubombo, Manzini, and Shiselweni).

Among the most delicate subjects in national life is land ownership. All land historically is vested in the monarch in trust for the country and distributed as community territory by the chiefs. But most of the region was alienated in the late 19th century as land grants to foreigners—as owners claimed but as lessees reported.

Trying to balance the rights of the Swazi with those of the concession holders was one of the first chores of the British crown when it took direct control of Eswatini (then known as Swaziland) in 1906. Little progress had been made by World War II; in 1907 it decided to set aside one-third of the nation for Swazi usage and let the concessionaires keep two-thirds.

The actual impulse came after independence when all the royal lands became national territory; soon afterward Britain agreed to fund the repurchase of about one million acres. The country bought other territory privately as well. Today, Swazi Nation Land comprises around two-thirds of Eswatini. The rest is held by individual title, however part of this is also under Swazi ownership, both nationally and personally.

Eswatini's Education

Precolonial missionaries brought schooling as a component of their activities, and their impact still shapes the educational landscape. Early as 1906, the Swazi country set up schools; some chiefs also founded what were regarded as "tribal" schools. But only after independence did the coverage of elementary and secondary schools start to rise sharply and allow more than eighty percent of the school-age population to enroll full-time.

This is why illiteracy is gradually decreasing. State education is not free, hence parents' principal financial outlay is school fees. Along with a university, there are facilities for vocational and industrial training as well as for teacher-training.

Health and Welfare

Church missions and industrial businesses serving large numbers of workers and their families provided the first push for health care. They founded rural clinics and two hospitals. Every bigger metropolitan center has private medical practitioners as well.

Food shortages, TB, intestinal infections, and respiratory disorders rank as main causes of sickness. Malaria has resurfaced as a serious illness after its apparent eradication in the 1950s, particularly in the Lowveld where a significant inflow of infected immigrant labor from Mozambique has occurred. With about one-fourth of the population affected, Eswatini was suffering from among the highest rates of HIV infection in the world by 2000.

Cultural Life

Though the money economy has brought about changes, by a high degree of literacy and basic education, and by constantly improving living standards and changing lifestyles, tradition still plays a significant role in Swazi society both at the national ceremonial level and in daily personal contacts. This represents the solidarity of the Swazi as one people under a traditional monarch and particularly their respect of the struggle of King Sobhuza II during the 61 years of his rule to recover their freedom.

The two biggest cultural festivals are the Umhlanga in August and the Incwala in December. Though spanned over six days, the Incwala is a much more complicated ritual of rejuvenating and strengthening the kingdom and the country, with songs and dances utilized only on this occasion.

It is often characterized as a first-fruits ceremonial. Lasting five days, the Umhlanga, often known as Reed Dance, gathers the unmarried girls and young women of the nation to cut reeds for the yearly repairs to the queen mother's village. It also represents the country's continuity throughout the massed ranks of young ladies and its solidarity. The queen mother conducts both ceremonies in the national capital.

Other rites link with custom weddings and with the community weeding and harvesting of the king's lands (and those of the chiefs). Usually, dances, singing, and traditional music accompany most celebrations. Simple in form, a kudu horn (impalampala) used for hunting or herding cattle, a calabash fastened to a bow (umakweyane) for love songs, the reed flute, played by little boys while herding, and rattles made of seedpods fastened to the wrists and ankles. But more common on the farm nowadays are the radio and record and tape players.

Part 3

Exploring Nature, Culture, and Tradition

Chapter 8

Heart of Eswatini's Monarchy

Lobamba, tucked away in the verdant Ezulwini Valley, is Eswatini's energetic political and cultural centre. Comprising the famous Lobamba Royal Village, this little but important town is the seat of the monarchy for the country. Featuring the Royal Kraal next to the Parliament building and other government offices, the hamlet offers a remarkable mix of history and modern administration.

It adds to Lobamba's appeal the small but fascinating National Museum. Inside its walls, guests can fully appreciate the rich tapestry of Eswatini's past, present, and natural surroundings. Exhibits feature traditional Swazi clothing together with thorough explanations of its cultural value. A few exhibits also show the natural fauna, therefore providing a window into the biodiversity of the nation.

A Wildlife Haven

One of the rare sites where visitors may see lions, elephants, and rhinos, Hlane Royal National Park is a haven for Eswatini's biggest herds of game. With the greatest population of breeding white-backed vultures in Africa, this park is a dream come true for bird watchers. Apart from observing animals, Hlane provides guided mountain biking excursions, cultural visits to surrounding Swazi towns, peaceful bird-watching walks, and exciting overnight jungle hikes.

Protecting Endangered Species

Mkhaya Game Reserve, about forty minutes south of Hlane Royal National Park, is a refuge for threatened animals. Originally created to protect white and black rhinos, this reserve also provides cover for buffaloes, giraffes, hippos, and a startling range of birdlife. The reserve's conservation initiatives make it absolutely vital for Eswatini to retain its natural legacy.

A Conservation Pioneer

Remarkably the first conservation area in Eswatini, Mlilwane Wildlife Sanctuary is still most visited game reserve. Ted and Elizabeth Reilly, environmentalists, founded the sanctuary and turned a farm into a vibrant 4,560-hectare wilderness. Mlilwane, tucked up among the Nyonyane Mountains, with a varied array of animals and more than 400 bird species. Being a non-profit refuge, it keeps motivating regional conservation initiatives.

A Landscape of Wonders

The biggest protected area in Eswatini, the Malolotja Nature Reserve stretches northwest. The Malolotja River flows throughout the reserve, cutting a course across the terrain and creating a sequence of waterfalls including the grand Malolotja Falls, the highest in the nation. From marshes and meadows to deep riverine forests, this varied environment covers The reserve explodes in color in spring and summer as wildflowers cover the ground, accentuating its already amazing landscape.

Chapter 9

Blend of Nature and Culture

The Mantenga Nature Reserve provides a special fusion of cultural legacy and natural beauty right in the center of Eswatini. The Mantenga Cultural Village, a living museum engulfing guests in Swati people's customs, is at its core. With activities like grinding grains and weaving mountain grass providing hands-on experience, guided visits expose the nuances of Swati culture. Captivating presentations of traditional music and dances that highlight Swati culture's vitality entertain guests.

Apart from its cultural value, the area provides a refuge for many species. Baboons, vervet monkeys, bush babies, porcupines, rock hyraxes, servals, leopards, and many species of antelope may be seen by visitors. The wealth of birdlife dancing over the reserve will satisfy aficioners. There are many choices for exploration; paths for mountain biking, hiking, and personal car animal viewing.

The most famous waterfall in the reserve is Mantenga Falls in Eswatini. Renowned for their amazing water volume, the falls offer a peaceful haven into the arms of nature and an amazing natural show.

Rich biodiversity

Not far from the Mozambique border, Mlawula Nature Reserve features a striking range of settings. From rolling green slopes and rich riverine forests to parched savannahs, the reserve is a patchwork of opposing biological zones. The steep topography running along the border accentuates the tough beauty of the place.

Among the many species found in the several habitats are wildebeests, kudu, impala, tortoises, and over sixty more species. With more than 350 species, birdlife thrives here along with a profusion of insects and an amazing range of flora. Both nature enthusiasts and explorers will find paradise on the reserve because to its distinctive topography and richness of species.

Riverside safari

The calm Mbuluzi Game Reserve sits on the banks of the Mlawula River, which is populated by crocodiles. This private reserve provides self-guided wildlife excursions whereby guests may explore at their own speed. Lack of big predators lets families and environment lovers enjoy the breathtaking scenery in peace.

There are many sightings of wildlife; giraffes, zebras, and nyalas are among the often seen species. Given the reserve's approximately three hundred species, birdwatchers will especially be delighted. Among them is the elusive Narina trogon, whose vivid plumage lashes the treetops with color.

Celebration of Maidenhood

The most well-known celebration in Eswatini, the Umhlanga Reed Dance Ceremony falls on the last week of August or the first week of September. Thousands of young Swati maidens from all throughout the country are assembling for this energetic cultural festival to deliver reeds to the Queen Mother and execute traditional dances.

Wearing vibrant clothing covered with animal skins and beads, the maidens move in unison to steady drumbeats. Attracting attendees from all around the world, the festival honors togetherness, purity, and tradition.

A Renewal Ritual

Among Eswatini's most important cultural events, the Incwala ceremony centers on royalty and rebirth. Deeply ingrained in history, this custom is observed during three weeks around the summer solstice.

The celebrations start with members of the Bemanti people collecting water during the new moon from main rivers. Then young men create a royal kraal at Lobamba, where the monarch of the country symbolically enjoys the first harvest products. The ceremony marks the togetherness of the Swati people and their connection to the land and monarchy by means of vibrant songs, dances, and group celebrations.

These locations and activities taken together create a clear image of Eswatini's rich cultural tapestry and breathtaking natural settings. Every provides a different view into the legacy of the country, hence Eswatini is a very interesting site for visitors.

Conclusion

Eswatini's history is a story of deep continuity and deliberate change. The threads of an ancient culture tapestry are carefully woven into the realities of modern development and government. Even though the world is changing quickly, its unique identity stays strong thanks to the tradition of strong monarchs and the unrelenting resolve of its people. The country's unique mix of traditional authority and modern systems shows that it is trying to protect its cultural identity while also dealing with important problems like economic disparity and health crises. With its beautiful landscapes and deeply rooted traditions, Eswatini doesn't just survive; it lives as a living link between tradition and progress, telling a unique story of strength and purposeful change.

Printed in Great Britain
by Amazon